No God, No Glory

A QUICK READER ON THE PRACTICAL PROOF OF GOD

No God, No Glory

A QUICK READER ON THE PRACTICAL PROOF OF GOD

Larry Bailey

No God, No Glory

ISBN 978-0-9819090-7-3

I dedicate this book to my wife, Gisella, and my daughters, Crystal and Coral. Their unconditional love has powered me through the difficult times.

Table of Contents

Introduction

I wrote this treatise primarily to please and honor God the Father. I also wrote it to please and honor my wife and children and my earthly father and mother. It turns out, however, that shortly after taking on this task, I began to see the project more as an effort to inspire myself and others to go to the mattress when it comes to reaching out for the Lord.

The existence of God has boggled the minds of philosophers and theologians for thousands of years. My purpose here is to cut through the clutter of the confusing assumptions and definitions made by many of these thinkers and present pragmatic proof of the existence of God from a simple practical perspective.

Chapter One

Prayer Is Real

Two actual events in my life illustrate the most important step you can take in building a relationship with God, and that is of course, prayer. When you pray with conviction, you get real practical results which inevitably serve to prove that God is living and responding to our needs.

The first event began after the long drive I took from the east coast of the United States to the west coast in search of my niche in life. During the early 1980's, I ventured to Hollywood California with the naïve notion that I would someday join the big top in the world of media entertainment. No such luck. Regardless, it was a wild adventure that I feel blessed to have survived.

I lived in a dusty roach motel on a seedy part of Hollywood Boulevard memorable only for its dimly lit rooms. I awoke from my bed one morning to feel the tremble of a significantly potent earthquake. When the ceiling started to fall, I jumped under the bed and eventually made it outside. I remember how cordial and concerned residents were toward one another as we ushered out of the building for safety. Even in Hollywood emergencies tend to bring people closer together.

Before long, a young fellow, whose name I can no longer recall, began to talk with me in front of the motel while we waited out the tremors. This guy whined and cried the blues so much that it made my own troubles seem almost tolerable. He told me he had no family to speak of, no work, no money, and was about to be thrown out of the motel where we were staying. I could tell by the emotion in his voice and the fear in his face that living homeless in the streets was not something he felt he could handle. Having just had a tough bout with it myself, I was sympathetic. I knew all too well the experience of being down and out in Beverly Hills and strolling Rodeo drive penniless.

In an effort to stop this young man's apparent propensity for suicide, I invited him to share in my bottle of Taylor's port. The only condition I gave him for sharing was that he should do all the talking. He was pleased with my offer and talked on and on as I sipped my wine contently. I listened to his problems and tried to help by asking him if he had ever tried this solution or that solution for any of his troubles and he would always answer, "Tried that, didn't work."

Eventually I told him there was one thing left he could try that would work if he were serious about it. By now he was pretty interested in what I had to say, but I made it clear to him that the next word to come from my mouth had to be taken as seriously as life and death itself and I made him promise not to take it lightly. After his promise to me, I said, "Pray!"

I told this troubled stranger what I had been telling myself over the last few days because I too was going through hard times. "Pray to the God of Abraham, Isaac, and Jacob," I told him. The young man was now very attentive and looked both amazed and rejuvenated by my advice. I also said that once he prays, he must truly believe that the Lord's hand will move all obstacles, because it is the believing and the faith that moves God to act.

I remember expressing to the young man how important it is to sincerely believe that the prayer will be answered. I kept repeating to him, "It is in the believing that the answer comes." At this point, the youngster anxiously stood up and said he was absolutely going to pray in the manner I described and took off.

By the time eight or nine days passed, I was so engrossed with my own problems that memories of the encounter faded into oblivion along with my ambition to stop by his motel room to check on his progress. I remember thinking that I would probably never run into the guy again and hoping things worked out for him.

Then, out of nowhere, while sitting in my car stopped at a traffic light on Hollywood Boulevard, I heard someone screaming my name from a distance. When the voice got closer I turned in my seat to see my earthquake friend pumping his bicycle pedals and waving his hand in a frantic effort to reach my car before the light changed to green.

"Larry!" he screamed. "Hey Larry!" He got to my car out of breath and in a deep sweat.

Still on his bike, he grabbed my car door to hold himself up as he gasped for words.

"I did it!" he said. "I prayed and it worked, it really worked!" Knowing that our time at the traffic light would be short and that our chances at another meeting were slim, he never stopped for my response. Instead he blurted out that God had answered his prayers by giving him a responsive family, a new job, and a new place to stay. I was so happy to hear his good news that I smiled, shook my head up and down, and gave him the thumbs-up hand signal to show my gladness because there was just no time to do anything else. Face to face he thanked me profusely, the light changed, and I drove off never to see the young man again. The joy I felt that day has never left me. The joy of being an instrument of God and a witness to His victory is indeed a joy like no other under the sun. Whatever you pray for with faith, you will receive. (Matthew 21:22) God exists. Behold His power.

Not long after this, I experienced another phase of financially difficult times. These hard times convinced me that being a college graduate with some work experience in radio and TV news was not enough to really become successful in L.A. I decided to accept the L.A. scene as a total bust and get back to the east coast to pursue more realistic goals. I would eventually sustain enough discipline, thanks to God and my Dad, to obtain a masters degree from Temple University while living and working in Philadelphia.

My next experience not only illustrates the power of prayer, but it also marks the point in my own life where I began to fully recognize the benefits of having faith. By the time I reached my thirties, I wanted a loving family. I decided it was time to pray like I had never prayed before. I felt it was time to put my love life in the hands of God instead of my own.

The first thing I wanted to do was to get it right. I wanted it to work and I knew it could work if I truly relied on all the faith I could muster. I kept thinking to myself that I should be able to plunge into this prayer thing with no sweat. After all, I was a believer from early on who grew spiritually each day as an altar server in the Episcopal Church. Yet, it was still hard to feel totally confident about what God really wanted for me at this particular time in my life.

I started by investigating the nuances of proper prayer. I discovered that there are benefits for including specificity in one's prayer. Being specific gives a prayer substance and makes it distinguishable in your mind from all other prayers. The more specifics placed in your prayer, the easier it is to recognize when it has been answered. Most importantly, specifics give glory to God.

So, with specifics in mind, I began praying for a lifelong female companion. I remember talking to God like I was talking to my earthly father or a good friend. I stated to God that He made me a natural man with the need for a natural woman. I also told God that He knew my heart as a whole and that I was no less deserving of a good woman than other men.

To plead my case further, I let God know that I felt neglected because I was a God-fearing law abiding citizen all alone in the world, while numerous high profile criminals with reputations for brutally murdering people had loving wives and children at home. After many years, I can still remember the specific names of the criminals that I listed in my prayer to show the contrast between my life and the lives of these other people.

Then, I begged the Lord, with all my heart and all my soul, for a good woman to love. I specifically requested that our mutual love for one another be genuine and last a life time.

During this period, I developed a fondness for Hispanic women simply because I found them to be relatively sincere and happy. I was also old school in my thinking and I was comfortable with their traditional values on the church, the family, and the home.

So I asked God specifically for a Hispanic woman with long dark black hair and beautiful dark eyes. I can not recall the other details that went into the mix of my request. I'm not even sure how long I waited to hear God's answer simply because I told myself from the beginning to pray, have faith, and then let it go. I was determined to leave everything totally in the hands of God. As such, I pretty much let the occasion slip into the back of my mind and eventually I forgot about it altogether. Looking back, I think it must have been faith coupled with having no time for reflection that somehow left me content with not hearing from God on the matter.

I remember at one point thinking how meeting and dating someone Hispanic would be pretty tough because I could not speak Spanish, nor did I live in or near a Hispanic neighborhood. Meeting my choice of woman was also difficult back in those days because almost everybody had their own neighborhoods and breaching those neighborhoods was often like going to another country without a passport. In time, I would come to understand that there are no obstacles for God.

God answered my prayer while I was attending graduate school in Philadelphia.

During the first week of the fall semester, I spotted what had to be in my mind the most beautiful young woman in the entire city sitting in my political science class. She had long beautiful black hair and dark eyes accentuated by a blue eye liner that made her look strikingly exotic.

After our class together, I waited for her to finish talking with the professor and approached her to introduce myself. Despite my inability to fully understand her heavy Puerto Rican accent, I managed to convey to her my wish for us to be friends. We exchanged phone numbers and not long after I was carrying her books and walking her home. We have been together ever since. Within three years of our first meeting we were wed and today we still share a great love and a great family life with our two wonderful daughters. God answered my prayer with flying colors. Behold the power of the Lord.

Chapter Two

Nothing Comes Before God

Atheists argue that we believers have not adequately explained what created God in terms of cause and effect. According to the atheists, believers credit the making of the universe to God and then contradict themselves by suggesting that God is somehow the exception to the cause and effect rule because He either created himself or He simply had no cause.

Regardless, when atheists pose this what created God question, which they believe can not be answered without contradiction, they are not disproving the existence of God; they are merely posing a question through which their limited perception provides no adequate answer.

Believers know better. We know when atheists pose this seemingly unanswerable question, they are really exhibiting nothing more than a fundamental ignorance of who God really is. If they really knew God, the question of who or what created God would never arise. Somehow they have developed a misguided concept of God. In short, atheists do not know God. Here are the pragmatic fundamentals the atheists systematically ignore.

The universe and mankind in his earthly form are finite. The laws of astrophysics, the cosmos, and thermodynamics have clearly defined the universe as finite with limited boundaries. The laws of chemistry and physics also support the notion that the universe had a beginning and is not, as many atheists contend, eternal or self-creating. The universe, comprised of matter, has not always been in existence nor did it propel itself into existence. It was created at some given point.

It is well established by science that the universe expands with time and continues to expand. The future is simply the expansion of the universe. As such, it follows logically to recognize that the past is a contraction of the universe that ultimately reduces all the way back to some beginning point. Thus, the universe is finite and was created at some beginning point by God.

The universe did not evolve by random chance, as the atheists contend. The universe is too well designed not to have resulted from an intelligent creator who created it with a purpose. Purposeful intelligent creation eliminates chance as the cause of what was created.

Believers argue life is precious and has purpose. Non-believers argue life can be precious, but it does not have to be purposeful. Atheists accuse believers of faulty reasoning and circular assumptions, but their arguments change nothing and prove nothing. Life either has purpose or it does not. In truth, life can only be precious if it's purposeful.

As it was written, in the beginning, man's immortal purpose was to live in God's paradise on earth in Eden, to care for the garden, and to extend that paradise of love to all the corners of the earth. See Genesis 2:15-17. When man broke God's law, God sent his son to earth to bear the burden of mankind's violations against divine law. God's wishes for mankind throughout the ages have never changed.

The purpose of life is to love and be loved in return. Non-believers are simply wrong and the material proof of God they so desperately seek actually lies before them and in front of their eyes, but they have no capacity to see.Frankly speaking, believers already know the conclusion to be proved-namely, that God exists, and therefore believers need no explanation of how we come to know this truth and no proof of any kind is necessary. Non-believers, on the other hand, operate outside the realm of spirituality, and as such, cannot know that God exists because no explanation or proof of His existence is possible for them.

Like the battered wife who refuses to file for divorce and accept the truth of her husband's disdain, non-believers are hard pressed to accept the truth of God although faced with boundless evidence.

The proof of the Creator is the created. The proof of the higher intelligence is the intelligence. Man is an intelligent creature who was created by the highest intelligence. Man, like the universe, is also too sophisticated to be the result of chance or the random flow of matter coming together over time.

The random motion of all the atoms of the universe could never produce a being of flesh and blood with the mental, physical, emotional, and spiritual capacity of the human species. Mankind is a remarkable being with a moral conscience that can not be explained merely in terms of the physical properties of matter or the electrical impulses inside or outside the brain. Moral conscience is better explained through the workings of a divine nonmaterial force we call the spirit.

Scientific theories on replication and natural selection operate to explain the material world, but say nothing about the nonmaterial reality. Further, theories on multiple and parallel universes convey more the atheist obsession with unsupported empirical data rather than a real understanding of what makes the world tick. A view of the world that ignores proven faith-based knowledge and considers only empirical data falls miserably short of the total reality.

The idea that all life on earth originated and evolved through a gradual series of mutations is purely a speculative hypothesis with no direct factual support. Fossil record shows each form or kind of plant and animal has a separate history from all the other forms and kinds. There is no trace of a common ancestor and certainly no link to any reptile, which is the supposed progenitor. Despite this lack of factual support, Darwinists treat their subject as if it were a self-evident axiom, when in truth; it has no more credibility than the tale of the tooth fairy.

Moreover, these physical and material theories prove little of the non-existence of God, but instead work thoroughly in proving the arrogance of atheist perspective. Our moral conscience, our ability to separate right from wrong, and justice from injustice, is the nonmaterial spirit residing in our physical bodies placed there by God.

Moral conscience could not have come from a random evolutionary process governed by survival of the fittest, kill or be killed, eat or be eaten. Moral conscience could only have come from God because survival of the fittest evolution could never produce any semblance of morality.

Further, if survival of the fittest had any real credence, we humans would have far more physical prowess than we do. You need only place a naked human being up against a lion in the jungle to easily see that on these terms, the lion will more than likely overcome the man. A man's intellect in this scenario could advance his chances for survival, but not necessarily in significant measure.

Logic also forces us to remember that just because something has survived does not necessarily mean that it is the most fit. A scant view of any standard tree of evolution model shows the older simpler animals at the bottom of the tree, while the recent and complex animals take the top. Placement on the model is problematic each time you find an animal that is so very old, yet so complex that it cannot be logically attached to the bottom of the evolutionary tree.

These cases are large in number and poke holes in the basic assumptions of Darwinism.

Atheists ignore the important distinction between what is finite and what is infinite. The universe is finite, but God is infinite. What is easily understandable for the believer is not understandable for the atheist. Atheists can not understand that God created the universe and the buck really does stop with Him. There is nothing greater than God. There is nothing beyond God. Therefore, there is no other entity that could have created God.

He created the heavens; note the word heaven in the plural form, and the earth- that's everything. From eternity to eternity, He is God. (Psalm 90:2)

In the beginning was the Word, the Word was with God, the Word is God.

In the beginning Jesus was with God. All things come through Him, and without Him nothing can come to be. (John 1: 1-3)

God, as an infinite spirit being, is allusive to our reality. (John 4: 24) He transcends human intelligence. He exists in a realm that is beyond what is fathomable. He is multi-dimensional and outside the dimensions of man. He is beyond space and time. He is supernatural.

The true source of who God is lies in the Holy Scriptures. In it, the nature of God as being outside space and time and also the Creator of space and time is made clear. One need only peruse 2 Peter 3:8, Psalm 90:4, Acts 1:7, and Jeremiah 23:22-24 to see this spelled out in no uncertain terms.

God is the ultimate Creator of all that exists, seen and unseen. He is eternal and He is one with eternity. He has always been and He will always be. He began time. He will end time. When He ends time, all matter in the universe and mankind will enter eternity with God.

God was not created because God is the Creator. God began the beginning because God is the beginning. He is infinite, and so He is also the end. In Revelation 22:13 we learn that He is the Alpha and the Omega, the beginning and the end, the first and the last.

In 2 Peter 3:10-13, Revelation 21: 1- 4, and 1 Corinthians 2: 7, we see the super nature of God revealed. Once we come to grips with who God really is, then it becomes obvious that nothing could have created Him.

Atheists are so far removed from God they even argue the ridiculous notion that an answered prayer is nothing more than coincidence and all unanswered prayers indicate that God is just simply no where to be found.

Like horses with blinders, atheists continue down the dark path with the same old contention that everything is just coincidence or chance and nothing has a reason or a purpose. How sad. We believers know everything happens for a reason and there is a purpose for everything under heaven. We know this by the Word of the scripture as a whole and not just by Ecclesiastes 3 alone.

Non-believers continue to stand by the theory of random chance and coincidence, but provide no real rational or practical evidence to support their view. They mistakenly believe that by offering up numeric postulates of probability to explain answered prayers, we will all suddenly be convinced that atheism is truth. Those of us connected to God understand that prayers can either be answered by God or they can simply fall outside the will of God. Make no mistake; it is God's will that must be done, not man's will.

Once again we must recognize that scientific knowledge is vastly incomplete. Science cannot explain how moral conscience emerges from the physical body and the neural activity of the brain. This inability of science to reconcile the material world with the nonmaterial or spiritual world leaves blatant gaps in the scheme of reality.

For the atheist, an incomplete science or a misunderstood conscience has nothing to do with the existence of God. For them, incomplete science and misunderstanding only means some science is undiscovered, but at some point in the future, without God, it will be completed by man's scientific research. In this secular light, God is relegated to nothing more than a genie in a bottle who conveniently substitutes for the gaps in science that have yet to be explained. In a nutshell, the story atheists believe is that mankind created God as the convenient answer to all the questions mankind cannot answer.

Those caught up in such dubious atheistic babble fail to see that God is not a replacement for our lack of understanding. God is understanding. God is not a substitute for our lack of knowledge. God is knowledge. What we come to know, and know as the truth, can only be known through God. It is only through God that man catches a glimpse of the truth because God is truth. By the proverbs of Solomon, we know that the fear of God is the beginning of knowledge.

God is love at the highest level. There is no love greater. God requests that we love one another because love is God. God is love. Anyone who loves comes from God and knows God. Those without love can not know God. (1 John 4: 7, 8) In John 3:16, we are informed that the Lord loved the world so much that He gave His only Son so that those who believe may gain eternal life.

God is love, peace, and truth. No man can know love, peace, or truth without God.

No man can determine right from wrong or good from evil without God.

Those who belong to God speak to others who listen because they too belong to God. Those who refuse to hear do not belong to God. This is how we distinguish between the spirit of truth and the spirit of deceit. (1 John 4: 6)

God created man. Man did not create God. God is too perfect, too good, and too demanding of us for us to have created. When man makes a religion, it embraces self-indulgence, not self-sacrifice.

Many of those who say we created God or say that God does not exist are often looking to excuse themselves from their own divine calling. They want to convince you and themselves that there is no God so they can rationalize or justify the secular world, and in some cases, even go so far as to fall to the level of the beast itself. (See Revelation 13)

I can recall a TV interview with a successful porn magazine publisher that caught my attention because it was so shocking to me. Boldly speaking on national TV this guy said, "I don't believe in God, but I believe in capitalism. It allows me to do anything I want for money and I make tons of it publishing filthy photos of the most disgusting acts imaginable and can you believe there are loads of crazy people out there eating it up like dogs on a bone and now I'm one of those guys who gets to laugh all the way to the bank."

This is a guy with the attitude, "There's no God, so I don't have to be Godly."

But because there is God, we all have to rise above the dark forces of the beast and be accountable for our actions in the here and now and in the hereafter. Man is distinct from all other living creatures because of his potential to rise to divinity and the kingdom of God. We are the only creatures made in His image, who carry His spirit, and can become one with Him.

Thus, the presence of the Lord does indeed explain the existence of moral consciousness with a practical ease and simplicity that is spiritually accurate as it gives glory to God. All else, including atheism, that is not of God, is falsehood and deceit cloaked in ambiguity and intellectual rhetoric.

Chapter Three

Christianity Over All Other Religions

It has been argued that religions across the world are mutually incompatible because each asks you to believe differently and each claims to be right and correct over the other. Some religions offer up many gods to worship, some claim only one, while others profess reincarnation or reject notions of heaven and hell altogether.

First, the presence of incompatible religions does not disprove God. Second, research in the larger scale religions show they have remarkable commonality in that they all place sovereign power in the hands of God. Third, even where religions significantly differ with man's interpretations over time, God remains who He is regardless of man's perceptions.

So which religion is the one to believe? They cannot all be true and thus they cannot all lead to God. The contention here is that Christianity has proven to be more historically accurate than all other religions in its embracement of truth, love, forgiveness, and faith. No other religion in the history of mankind has made more impact on the moral character of the world's people than Christianity.

No other religion has fulfilled prophecy with total accuracy through the Bible and no other focuses on the most acclaimed Messiah in all of history and the performance of His miracles.

Factual history reveals the most famous figure of all time, worthy beyond compare, is Jesus Christ, the deity in the flesh. His impact on human history is so profound, we measure time itself with His birth. The time before Christ was born is known as BC or before Christ. The time after His birth is marked anno domini or AD. The historic eye witnessed accounts of Christ and Christianity tells the story of the one true God-the God of Abraham, Isaac, and Jacob.

The thickest swamp of atheist dogmatism is easily swept away by simple truth. There is only one God, and somehow, each and every one of us must come to recognize for ourselves what the Egyptian pharaoh finally recognized about Moses-and that is, his God is God. There is only one way to God and salvation and that is through Jesus Christ because He is who He said He was-God in the flesh. Jesus and God are one. (John 10:30)

Like no other religious leader, Christ claimed to be God and proved it through His supernatural and miraculous deeds. These unparalleled words and actions were witnessed and recorded in the Scriptures for transmission to future generations.

No other religious leader and no other being in human history can match the accomplishments of the Lord Jesus Christ. He healed diseases, restored sight to the blind, cured deafness and paralysis, fed the multitude, walked on water, and raised himself from the dead. No other in history has conquered death. Not Buddha, not Confucius, not Muhammed, not Krishna, only Jesus.

Upon review of the other systems of religion with a reasonable eye, one is left unfulfilled on the concepts of life after death and the character of God. This is due mainly to the fact that they offer inconsistent and illogical notions on reincarnation, idol worship, polygamy, and the persecution of women and people in general that are just unacceptable.

There is only one true religion because there is only one true God. Only in Christianity could man's soul be restored to salvation through Christ's resurrection and only God Himself could make such an option available to us.

If one concludes that holy documents held sacred by the group he was born into are true, but those held sacred by the group he was not born into are false, then it could be said that taking such a position amounts to arrogant provincialism.

On the other hand, one might also argue that none of this is relevant. After all, the arrogance of any contention or the physical and geographic location of any human being to any particular historic event, past or present, does not change what the truth actually is.

The truth is perfect and absolute. It can not be partisan, bias, or arrogant. It can not vary with perception or vary from individual to individual because then it would contradict itself. The truth can not contradict itself because then it would not be truth. The truth can not be subjective or whatever we want it to be at any given time.

All religions can not be true. Their contradictions make this clear. One religion, however, can be true and is true. Truth is truth and that which falls into the category of truth falls there for no other reason than because it is, in fact, true. There is only one true God-the God of Israel. There is only one true faith-the faith in our Lord and Savior, Jesus Christ.

The scriptures make it clear that we can call on God anywhere, anytime, and He will move His mighty hand. After all, who else would have the power to really help us? No one but God can help us.

There is no salvation in anyone else, there is no other in the whole world given to men by whom we are to be saved. (Acts 4:12) Jesus asks us to turn to Him and be safe because He is God and there is no other God. (Isaiah 45:22)

When you call on the Lord and pray to Him, He will listen to you. When you look for Him, you will find Him. When you seek Him out with your heart, you will find Him with you. (Jeremiah 29: 12-14)

Chapter Four

What Suffering is Really About

Most atheists argue that the existence of massive suffering the world over is proof of the non-existence of God. Simple observation shows nothing could be further from the truth.

Suffering is the result of the transgressions man makes against God and the natural order of the universe He created. As man persists in these transgressions, he must suffer the consequences. We all know, believers and non-believers alike, that God has rules. If we ignore the rules or break the rules, we can not expect God to intercede with hypocrisy and prevent us from facing the consequences because then the very law of God and the order of the universe would mean nothing, stand for nothing, and allow for nothing, including the truth.

Suffering is really not about God's neglect of us, it is about our neglect of God. The rules and laws of God are but simple truths that combine to form the natural order of the universe. For example, if you smoke too much, lung cancer may plague your health. If you abuse alcohol, you may suffer a damaged liver. The pollution of the earth's water will cause disease to follow. Items on the list of human suffering appear endless, but nothing on such a list is inconsistent with a loving and merciful God.

God's love for us is not unlike the love we earthly fathers feel for our children. The love I have for my daughters is unconditional, but it still comes with consequences for not doing what is right, good, and just.

Suffering does indeed come from transgression, but it is also brought forth to fulfill and sustain God's work. The work of God, no matter how ingenious one thinks they are, can never be fully understood by mortal man.

Regardless, the notion of suffering for salvation is illustrated in the scriptures when the disciples asked Jesus, "Master, who did the sin, the man, or his parents, that he was born blind?" Jesus answered, "Neither the man, nor his parents: but the works of God must be made manifest in him."

Somehow, someway, this man's particular plight toward God is better served through blindness than through physical sight. We believers know that it is better to walk blind with God than to walk in full sight without Him.

In essence, suffering and pain is necessary for life purpose and life sustenance. If one could not feel the pain of a severed artery, one would fail to seek medical attention in time and bleed to death. In this case, pain is a good thing because it serves as a warning against a greater threat. The physical pain of suffering warns us, protects us, and enables us to survive until the cause of our pain can be eliminated.

We have to understand that feeling pain is consistent with universal law and is, in fact, healthy. The inability to feel pain is, of course, unhealthy. It is also unhealthy and inconsistent with the order of the universe for people not to feel compassion.

The Third Reich for example, sent many innocent people to their deaths because its members had no capacity to feel for others. Yet, the death of innocent people during the holocaust may also serve to remind the world that it needs God and His compassion. Man sometimes undergoes tragedy to find and recognize God. Suffering is a necessary component in the entire scheme of things set in motion by God and it can only be fully understood by God. Our job is to go with the flow-God's flow. The flow brings the passage of time, death comes, suffering and pain ends, then it is on to God.

Whether we live, or die, we are the Lord's. (Romans 14:8) It is foretold that God will wipe away all tears; there will be no more death, sorrow, or pain: and all that we once knew will pass away. (Revelation 21: 4)

Chapter Five

Faith and Reason Together

Man has not the capacity to make sense of God nor is God supposed to draw clear in our senses. Imagine an ant trying to make sense of a man stepping along side an ant hill. An ant can not come any where near the realities and understandings of man. In the same light, God is not about what makes sense to us. God can never be totally about what makes sense to us because he is beyond our senses. The scriptures remind us that our wisdom is but foolishness and folly to God. (1 Corinthians 3:19)

God is not what we as made creatures can fathom about our maker or put together from our science and technology. God is about faith and spirit. What is amazing and even more interesting is that the amount of faith we need is so very little. It is written, faith the size of a mustard seed can move mountains. (Matthew 17:20)

What it amounts to is that with a little faith and a little common sense, one can walk with the Lord. This sounds like a good deal to me. What about you? Just a little faith and reason will get you where you need to go. Suppose you were at a casino involved in a high stakes wager over the very existence of God. If you had to bet on whether God exists or not, all it would take to make the right choice is a little common sense and a tad bit of faith. You would literally have to be a fool to bet that God does not exist because to do so is to lose absolutely everything. The atheist is in a no-win situation for all reality.

When you bet on the almighty power of God, the maker of heaven and earth and the universe, you win all there is to win, up to and including eternal life. If by some strange and unrealistic quirk, God were not around, believers betting on God have nothing to lose. The believer is in the win-win situation for all reality.

What many fail to understand in this age of misinformation is that your belief, or your lack of it, is the ultimate criteria determining life eternal or simple death.

The gamble is between never-ending life and simple physical death. It is not between never-ending life and eternal torture. Hellfire is not the Word of God. Make no mistake; the idea of eternal torture is repugnant to God. In truth, his maximum punishment for sin is to revoke the gift of life. The wages of sin is death, but it is not eternal fire and damnation. (Jeremiah 7:31, Romans 6:7)

So when you gamble with your eternity, and it is your eternity, remember the stakes are high. Making the right choice must be rational and most of all, heart-felt and genuine, otherwise, it is merely an empty vow. Most important of all, we must remember that God is all merciful and all loving, and not all vengeful.

Faith and reason together will bring you to God. Separate them, as the secular world attempts to do, and mankind falls into the rut of unhappiness and functional madness.

Mankind can only be in synch with the universe and God when the physical, mental, emotional, and spiritual components of his being are interconnected and balanced. If we through our own free will choose to upset the balance of these components, we are inevitably choosing to move further away from God.

What is good, moral, and Godly comes from God and God alone. It does not come, as atheists contend, solely from man's reasoning ability. Reasoning, experimentation, and scientific progress can not on their own enable mankind to obtain morality simply because science asserts a limited truth. Spiritual knowledge or faith-based knowledge is the true enabler of morality in man because this kind of knowledge is unlimited in its depth and breadth of reality. Spiritual knowledge supersedes the dimensions of any empirical data that can be formulated by man. Spiritual knowledge is ultimate truth, empirical knowledge is limited truth. In short, we must first obtain spiritual knowledge before scientific knowledge can make any real sense- not the other way around.

As quiet as it is kept, God is a self-evident truth. We believers know this through our life's spiritual, physical, mental, and emotional contact with the Holy Spirit. It is this contact and faith that makes believers really who they actually are-the children of God.

Chapter Six

We Know God Exists

Atheists need to start speaking for themselves instead of everyone else. They contend that none of us actually knows God exists. This is wrong. Some of us do actually know. I am one of them. So what is knowing? This question opens a can of worms better left for philosophers, but practically speaking, to believe is not necessarily to know. You can believe your death will come at old age and not actually know that you are going to die in a car accident before your sixteenth birthday. Still, others may intuitively come to know precisely when their hour of death is to arrive and do nothing to prevent it because they know it is their time. Suffice it to say, it is not in believing that we come to know, it is in knowing that we come to believe.

We know of God from God Himself, Jesus Christ, who spoke to the apostles of His deity. This knowledge was written from eyewitness accounts and passed to others throughout the generations. The extraordinary miracles Jesus performed were public events involving thousands who were either physically nourished or physically healed.

It is practically impossible to keep this kind of public news from spreading across the globe and down through time.

History's greatest minds support the notion that God exists over the notion that He does not simply because they see God as too powerful not to be taken seriously. Current research among universities, research facilities, and industrial laboratories indicate that at least 8 out of every 10 scientists follow a religious faith. This link between scientists and faith is likely due to the long standing scientific and archeological accuracy of Biblical reference.

Let it be known, God is who He is- The Lord Almighty. He is everywhere, in the wind, and in us. He is what is and there is nothing else. God exists and we know it!

Despite the illusion that existence results from a multitude of forces, the truth of existence is, there is nothing outside of God. God is not one of many factors in the understanding of existence, He is the only factor. It is His will and His will only that commands all existence. We know God exists because He is within us giving us His power. This power grows through virtue and prayer. It is virtue and prayer that brings the human soul closer to the holiness of the Holy Spirit. When human beings turn away from virtue and prayer, spiritual holiness subsides and man removes himself from true peace. Only God can smother the drudgery of day to day life and replace it with the pristine peace of heaven on earth.

Chapter Seven

The World is Enough

The world and its condition should be enough to convince you that history is a reflection of the conflict between good and evil. Inevitably, people take one side or another through the free-will choices they make during their life time. The camps are clearly divided.

The few people of the world with extreme power and wealth are engaged in the systemic oppression of those without it. The old news that roughly two percent of the world's population owns half the world's wealth and resources should have been disturbing enough. Yet, today, the bounty of the rich has grown to even more. Current studies show the rich continue to get richer and the poor continue to grow poorer. The powerful and select few control the masses. They own everything and they control everything.

On an international scale, they own and control the means of production, the sources of information and education, the media, the means of creating and distributing income, all the military and police forces, the legal system, the banks, and much of the world's manpower.

These select few of about twelve families rule the rest of the world from power derived generally through ungodly means and their activity has been chronicled in Scripture as the activity of man just before the dawn of God's return to earth. As prophesized in the Bible, victory over these despots will come only through God's divine intervention.

It is right, then, that the solution of mankind's ills should come from God, after all, who else would have the power? Who else would have the power to heal a culture that breeds debauchery, war, hatred, disease, and poverty? It is this culture of death that has saturated the media and crept into our lives by strangling moral consciousness to the point of no return. It is this media that promotes having it all, at any cost, even if it is illegal-so long as you do not get caught.

The world is in a period of neoliberal economic integration-better known as globalization. Although it was supposedly started to make things better, it has failed miserably to prevent the widening gap of disparity between the poor and the prosperous.

This is probably due to the fact that those select few in power over the world truly want this disparity.

In the least developed countries, people fall further and further behind and deeper into poverty, while in the developed countries we see an explosive growth in the wealth of the mega-rich. This explosive growth in wealth has little to do with artful investment or wise business dealings, rather it is more the result of doing anything and everything to squeeze out the middle class and the poor and it has now become a world wide phenomenon.

Leading sociologist Jan Pieterse explains that the world's cake is getting gobbled up by a tiny group of gluttons while literally billions of people are being deprived of even the smallest of crumbs. Despite this evil disparity, power elites continue to call for more inequality by proposing more "hands-off the market" policy.

This ever-widening gap of disparity is vast beyond historical precedent and it breaches the code of human morality to the point of being grotesque. American culture has become entrenched in secularism to the point where no one condemns a reality TV show like Mob Wives. People connected to illegal activity should not be able to reap the illustrious benefits of celebrity and fortune by parading in front of a camera. The message media is sending through programming of this nature is wrong. TV shows on the wives of firefighters, social workers, teachers, or environmentalists would serve a greater good.

This is the state of our world. It is an immoral state that can only be reversed by the Almighty. God is the only spirit person in existence who can resolve the world's deepening plunge into the abyss of darkness.

Regardless, believers need not fear. Prophecy reveals that although the culture of death will bring the demise of many, it will bring new life with God to those who walk in faith and keep His Word. Judeo-Christian heritage is embedded with descriptions of mankind's struggle between good and evil. This struggle is destined to rage on until the Holy War of Armageddon is sparked by the forces of the Anti-Christ. These same forces have been linked to the New World Order. Once this war brings us to the brink of destruction, God returns to save the world and prove in no uncertain terms that He is the one and only true God. When mankind's reign on earth is put to an end, God's reign on earth begins. God is in control. In His time, He will intervene. "...Thy kingdom come, thy will be done..."

Chapter Eight

The Ultimate Proof

One must be able to comprehend the supernatural before one can comprehend God. The supernatural can be described as that which impacts on nature in a prolific manner and is beyond mankind's control, ability, and understanding.

Nature belongs to God and is subject to His will. God wills things to operate with a high degree of consistency to reduce chaos and allow human beings to live and make choices. Oil burns when you light it because God wills it to burn. God could just as easily will water to burn, simply because nature has no independent reality.

God is clearly a supernatural spirit being. God in the flesh is Jesus. The ultimate proof of God is in the miracles He performs. It is impossible to separate God's identity from His miracles. It is in these miracles that we come to distinguish God from all other beings. Through miracles, God proves that He is God.

People who disbelieve in God have an inadequate and unrealistic view of the supernatural, making belief in miracles impossible. These skeptics say there is no such thing as the supernatural, but they really establish nothing. After all, not one of them holds convincing evidence that there is no God.

On the other hand, we have the greatest story ever told. It is a story supported by historical evidence that weighs overwhelmingly in favor of God's miracles as actually occurring-giving credibility to His existence and His omnipotence. Jesus would have drawn little attention had He not healed the sick and raised the dead. In ancient times there was no mass media to carry communication globally within a matter of seconds. The truth is, after almost 20 centuries later, very few people would have heard of Jesus Christ today had it not been for the supernatural miracles He orchestrated during His brief three and a half year ministry.

In essence, it is God's miracles that support His identity and establish His authenticity.

God performs miracles so that we can identify Him and so that we will know that He exists. Miracles, then, are an overt and powerful witness to God's identity and existence. People reject them at their peril.

Miracles separate God from man. Jesus' miracles were meant to convince people of His deity. His miraculous deeds were so enormous in number that a listing could not fit on the pages of several oversized books. His good deeds were so spectacular that even those who actively sought to end His life attested to His possession of supernatural power.

Jesus' miracles convinced the world that He was more than a man and clearly worthy of worship as the one and only true God. His miracles also gave us insight into the heart of God because when Jesus committed himself to act, He moved with great compassion on behalf of not just various individuals, but also on behalf of the multitudes.

When He fed the hungry, He fed multitudes. When He healed the sick, He healed multitudes. Jesus encouraged all who would listen to look beyond His words and check out His deeds. He stated, "Believe the works, that you may know and believe that the Father is in Me, and I in Him." God was telling us how to distinguish Him from all other things-by His miracles. (John 10: 38, Isaiah 43:11-13)

Through eyewitness testimony we know that Jesus gave sight to the blind, restored and reconstructed crippled limbs, commanded the creatures, healed lepers, calmed the sea and storms, fed and healed thousands, cast out demons, walked on water, and raised Himself and others from the dead. Most of these miracles were accomplished by the mere utterance of a word. It is these unparalleled feats of all time that make Him, without question, the most significant figure in human history. It is these same feats that prove He is God. (John 14:6, Matthew 10:32)

Nonbelievers erroneously claim that God's miracles have been embellished and increased as time goes by in the same way Greek mythology has been exaggerated. The difference, of course, is that in the real world there is a real God who caters to real men, real women, and real children with real needs-like curing leprosy, or hunger, or thirst.

The truth of the matter is that the writers of the Scriptures actually decreased the number of miracles as time went on. Instead of adding more countless miracles, they preferred to focus on Christian teachings and lessons. Unlike mythology, the accounts of the Gospels, including the miracles, reflect the actual history of Jesus that remains to this very day-undisputable. Although parts of the Bible were written as early as the time of Moses, the Gospels are particularly relevant because they were first written some thirty years after the death of Jesus.

At a time when Jews considered making the claim to be God the worst of heresies punishable by death, Jesus made that very claim. Jesus knew He was God, taught that He was God, allowed Himself to be worshipped as God, and proved He was God by His miracles. More importantly, Jesus allowed Himself to be killed on the cross to redeem mankind simply because He is the all loving and all merciful one true God. Jesus really is God.

The greatest of God's miracles was His resurrection. Those that deny it happened have historically put forth a set of baseless and pathetic arguments that amount to outright absurdity. The truth is that it happened. The evidence to support it is far more persuasive because it is, by nature, true and because it comes ultimately from God Himself.

Jesus was once asked about how long the people were to be kept in suspense regarding His identity. Jesus said they had been told but they refused to believe. He also told them that His works done in His Father's name testify to Him. (John 10: 24)

The gospels point out that the disciples witnessed the death and resurrection of Jesus and presented the evidence of the resurrection by exposing an empty tomb. Some of the Roman guards also witnessed these events. Keep in mind that at the point in which the disciples had declared the body of Jesus as risen, Roman guards would have been deployed to every sector of the empire to find the body and dispel the authenticity of the risen Lord. No scourged or beaten body was ever found. The tomb was empty because Jesus left it. Furthermore, the likelihood of deception on the part of the disciples is highly improbable and illogical simply because faking death and resurrection from death is impossible.

Even if it could be faked, no Roman guard has ever been known to have conspired with the disciples in order to fabricate such a prolific event. In essence, the Christians and the Romans both accepted the empty tomb of Jesus as significant support for His rise from the dead.

Christians and Romans alike also accepted the notion that a stone weighing over two tons was placed in front of the tomb to seal it closed and then later rolled away for opening. A look at the tombs of the period in Jerusalem today show they were built with a down hill track to the tomb's entrance. This track or groove was cut in rock to allow for a stone of tremendous size to roll down to the tomb's door with minimal resistance. Perhaps one could argue that the tomb was sealed by twenty or thirty able bodied men using this track to roll the stone down, but rolling the stone up would be next to impossible. Believers say the stone could only be removed by supernatural power. It is written in the Bible that an angel of the Lord rolled the stone back. Short of the totally absolute, which is the case for much of what mankind perceives, there is always room for faith, and faith is good, because it gives glory to God. (Mark 16:1-6)

It is Jesus Himself who tells us the truth. The truth is that with faith in God, we can move mountains into the sea. If you believe with no doubt that you have received the things you asked for in prayer, God will provide them for you. (Mark 11:22-24)

The people of 2000 years ago were no different from the people of today when it comes to the deity of Christ. In a larger sense, they were probably worse than today's doubters because they witnessed the most blatant miracles of God firsthand, and still did not wholly believe. Even the disciples sought more proof from the returned Jesus by requesting that He show them the scars from His hands and feet. Inevitably, they came to realize the truth of God's presence on earth in Jesus.

The apostle Paul wrote within twenty five years after the resurrection that the risen Jesus was seen by over 500 eyewitnesses. The stories of these eyewitnesses are chronicled in the Bible. These eyewitnesses provide more evidence of Jesus as Lord than was provided during the Renaissance to show the world was round instead of flat. By modern standards in a court of law, evidence to this degree is considered overwhelming, to say the least. Many notable historians today assert that gospel narratives are close to infallible in showing that Jesus revealed Himself after crucifixion at many different times to many different people under many different circumstances. See Mark 16:14-19, John 20: 26-29, Matthew 28:16-20, and 1 Corinthians 15:4-6.

God can not be denied. Ample research and study of ancient history makes it clear cut that the early disciples of Christ suffered heinous persecutions and deaths. Yet none of these over 500 devoted brothers and sisters ever denied His deity or resurrection even in the face of death.

His inner circle of disciples was especially devoted. Some of them met death in Syria, some in Rome, some in Israel, others in Italy, India, and Babylon. Separated from one another, they each testified that they had seen the resurrected Christ. They could have easily denied Him and spared their own lives. There would have been no consequences and no one would be the wiser. Instead they chose the grueling agony of martyrdom. Check out how they suffered.

Matthew was killed by a sword stabbing in Ethiopia. Luke was hanged in Greece.

John was boiled in oil, but miraculously survived to write the last book of the New Testament around 96 A.D. Mark was dragged by horses to his death in Egypt. When Peter was sentenced to death, he felt unworthy of dying in the same manner as Christ, so he demanded that he be placed up side down on the cross.

James was thrown off the pinnacle of a church temple and then clubbed to death in Jerusalem. This was the same pinnacle where the Temptation of Christ took place.

Andrew was bludgeoned by soldiers and crucified. Bartholomew, also known as Nathaniel, was flayed like a fish until his death. James the Great was beheaded in Jerusalem. Paul was tortured and beheaded by Emperor Nero in 67 A.D. Thomas was speared to death in India.

Jude was killed by arrows. Matthias was stoned and then beheaded.

There is only one true God. This is stated unequivocally in the Scriptures. He formed the light, and created the darkness. He makes things well or creates woe. He does all things. He made the earth and created mankind to walk upon it. His hands stretched out the heavens. (Isaiah 45: 5, 7, 12)

Chapter Nine

God Owns Forgiveness

Who else but God could demand we love even our enemies and do well to those who hate us? Who else but the living God Himself could tell us? "Forgive, and you will be forgiven." Only God can forgive our sins. Jesus proves He is God when He forgives sin because no other being could have such power. No being has the right or the authority to forgive or remove sin except God Himself. Forgiveness may be a quiet unseen supernatural power of God, but it is as significant as the parting of the Red Sea because it opens the door for an intimate and everlasting relationship with the Lord.

God grants us peace and salvation. What other being has this kind of power? God loved the world so much that He gave His only Son so that whoever believes in Him may have eternal life. (John 3:16)

The enormous extent to which God goes to show His mercy and forgiveness toward mankind is present throughout the ages. Perhaps the most powerful evidence of His mercy and forgiveness can be found during His excruciating torture on the cross.

Jesus was beaten and marred beyond human likeness by Roman soldiers and religious leaders, yet in this pitiable condition, He prayed, "Father, forgive them, for they know not what they do."

Who else but God Himself could partake in actually saving the very people who had put him to death? Here God has left us with the greatest example of forgiveness in history and a standard for us all to live by. The bottom line, there is no sin too great for God to forgive.

In Jeremiah 33:8, God reminds us that He invented forgiveness and that nobody does it better than He. "They sinned against me, but I will wash away that sin. They did evil and turned away from me, but I will forgive them." Let there be no mistake about it, God owns forgiveness.

Chapter Ten

God Delivers

I taught at a number of colleges and high schools over the years. Although I also held different government and media positions that were interesting, it was teaching that brought me to a new awakening when it comes to God and the world we currently live in.

We all know that many of life's experiences are just that-simply life's experiences. Then there are others that are absolutely mind-blowing scary like the one I had teaching at a state college in Florida. It was as if one day I just suddenly woke up in the nightmare of a different world-a twilight zone, a world that did not love God. It was a world I did not want, but there it was, and the only thing I could ask myself was-how did we get to this point? When did the nightmare become reality?

This nightmarish reality began for me in the last class before the final exam during the fall semester of 2011. I wrapped up an extensive introductory course in government and politics by passing on a message of hope for the future in spite of the recurring theme of corruption historically present in the system.

I instructed the class on how the founding fathers tried to impede tyranny by establishing a government based in Christian principles. To illustrate the point, I spoke of Jefferson's words from the Declaration of Independence, "... They are endowed by their Creator with certain unalienable rights..." These rights are divine. I spoke on Benjamin Franklin's request that prayer be said before each Constitutional Convention meeting. I discussed Lincoln's consecration at Gettysburg and how it described government for the people and by the people as one that must be under God. I talked about the words printed on our money, "In God we Trust," and the words of our pledge of allegiance to the flag, "One nation, under God."

I asked the class to consider the words of the second president of the United States, John Adams, "We have no government armed with power capable of contending with human passions unbridled by morality and religion." I inject that George Washington, during his farewell address, stated, "... Reason and experience both forbid us to expect that national morality can prevail in exclusion of religious principle."

I also spoke on what early patriot Benjamin Rush believed. He argued that a republic had to have religion as its foundation because without it there can be no virtue, and without virtue there can be no liberty, and without liberty there can be no republic.

In essence, firmly embedded in the political program of the founding years, including the writing of the Constitution of 1787 itself, there is a political philosophy intimately related to Christian theology.

The founders believed that good character was vital to the health of the government and the nation as a whole. America's first Supreme Court Justice John Jay served as the president of the American Bible Society.

I instructed the class on how John F. Kennedy addressed Americans in his inaugural speech with the words, "God's work must truly be our own." The Supreme Court, after studying the issue in detail, conclusively declared this nation to be a Christian nation in the Trinity Decision of 1892.

This case established that at least 90 to 95 percent of the founders were practicing Christians who believed religion was actually vital to the success of government and not something to be feared as suggested by atheistic interpretations of the first amendment.

The most radical of these interpretations is the implied metaphor known as separation of church and state. By this erroneous and absurd interpretation, we are supposed to believe that church and state and faith and reason can not and must not operate together.

The states passed laws based on this flawed Supreme Court interpretation of the first amendment. This is a grave mistake. For man's reason can not operate outside the realm of faith. The church and the state can not realistically be separated because they are both comprised of men and mankind can not be separated from spiritual reality.

As such, let it be clear, that our unalienable rights are 'endowed by our Creator'-not by the state. The words of President Kennedy make it plain, "The rights of man come not from the generosity of the state, but from the hand of God."

Laws, federal or state, which curtail religious freedom or try to separate spirituality from all other areas of life, are wrong. Separation of church and state is wrong because they can not be separated. Separation of church and state is also wrong because the state created it from a false interpretation of the constitution. At no place in the constitution does it state that the church and the state must be separate and at no place in the constitution is it even rationally implied.

Since the late 1940's, the Supreme Court has systematically struck down any activity resembling adherence to Christianity all in the name of "freedom of religion." In reality, these decisions promote atheism and open the door of persecution for Christians.

If George Washington were to read these decisions, he would probably be repulsed at the audacity of the court to intellectually unravel morality before our very eyes by gradually stripping out Christian principles. He would roll over in his grave to see what is going on today because he believed that secularism is the foundation of tyranny.

I instructed my students to recognize that the founders of the country believed democracy was all about placing the rights of individuals over the rights of the state and the best way for them to support their position was to use the Bible. I gave historic facts on the number of languages the book has been translated in, when the book was first printed, and its top selling capacity throughout the ages.

After describing the three largest religions in the world and providing a breakdown of global population numbers and percentages for each, I presented Jesus as the historic figure He was with simple facts-like who He is known as, how we mark time on the basis of His life, and the controversial views of the man so as to give students some understanding of how His story influenced the founding fathers in the set up of this country's government. By using only the facts, I was able to give students some sense of why the founders relied on the Bible to form the government.

Christian principles were important in the founding of our republic and the framing of our governmental institutions. Many academicians today believe they will be equally important in the maintenance of our government.

The majority of my students were fascinated and thrilled to receive different facts on the foundation of American government. Keep in mind that by now my students have already grown accustomed to open discussion on just about every political issue one can imagine. By this time, almost every emotional land mine in this field of study had been stepped on.

Regardless, in this one particular class, one female student and her male companion were apparently not fascinated at all with what I had to say. Toward the close of the lecture, they slammed their books together and walked out of the class in an unmistakable posture of protest and defiance.

Offended by their abrupt exit, I told these two students that it was their choice to leave class and remain uninformed. Within hours of the incident, I received a recorded message from my immediate supervisor stating that he was receiving complaints about my class. I called him back to talk personally, but I could not reach him. At this point I felt there was no need to be too concerned. I was an Outstanding Adjunct Faculty Award Nominee for 2009 and I felt confident about my teaching skill and performance. I also felt that I had done nothing wrong.

The following day I received a call from the college social science Dean. He told me that complaints were made to my immediate supervisor regarding my discussion of God in class and that it was recorded. The Dean then requested that I explain the situation. After doing so, he assured me that a committee to include myself would be formed to set standards on teaching the link between government and religion in order to avoid complaints in the future. He closed the call with the words, " I hope it doesn't go viral."

A day or so later another call came from the Dean. In this somber call he stated that an audio portion of my lecture could be heard on you tube and directed me to a site so that I could see and hear for myself. I was told not to expect another call until after his investigation and we hung up.

I then immediately pulled up the site. I was shocked. The magnitude of viciousness perpetuated against me by these two students was finally dawning on me. These two apparently atheist students walked out of my class and went straight to a computer to create a special website devoted to soliciting complaints against me for discussing God in class. On the site they placed the email address of my boss and requested that complaints be made to him and that he do something about my alleged preaching. Two days later I received a final call from the Dean. He stated simply, "You have been removed from the schedule for next semester."

I was blown away and heartbroken over never having the chance to meet with anyone regarding the incident as initially promised. After two decades in the field, the Dean's insensitive over the phone dismissal was capped by the cynical words, "I hope this doesn't cramp your style." The loss of thousands of dollars is a major cramp for anyone in this recessionary age. The Dean then closed his call with, "Happy Holidays!"

I followed up with a faxed statement and an email stating the audio was taken out of context, but they were ignored.

Looking back on the whole affair, I am still mortified at how my reputation as a good teacher dwindled to nothing based on the word of just two students. Not only was the posting illegal in that they recorded the segment without my consent, but it was also unjustified because anyone who has ever taken my class knows that it is focused wholly on government and could never be mistaken for religion. As far as I am concerned, giving students the facts is not and can never be proselytizing.

The incident here along with other world events is convincing proof that the opponents of God are at work. Fortunately, the opponents of God can not defeat God or mankind, for we are God's greatest creation. He will return before we are too far gone because we are also His greatest love. Regardless, the near death of our culture becomes apparent by the fact that teachers who suggest we are related to monkeys are permitted to speak freely, while teachers who suggest we are related to God are silenced.

I began to pray incessantly. My prayers were focused on preserving my family and finding work as soon as possible. This, I knew, would take God's intervention. After all, in the second highest unemployment state in the nation, nothing short of a miracle would get me a new job. After my prayers, God delivered.

I was notified by phone on December 17, 2011 not to return to the campus. Just days later, on December 24, 2011, I began my first day on a new job providing publications to retail outlets across the region. All it took was for my youngest daughter to tell a friend my story and before I knew it, her friend's father hired me. My daughter's concern and the hand of God did the trick. Today, I pray for the two lost souls who could not tolerate their teacher giving glory to God. Perhaps one day they will understand that with God all things are possible, but without Him, you can do nothing. (Matthew 19:26)

In summary, I say to all those who shriek over Bible thumping-let the Bible be thumped some more. We must not forget that although God is loving and merciful, we are all subject to His will and judgment. Heed the word of the Lord.

The Lord states that whoever is not with Him is against Him. Every sin and blasphemy of the people will be forgiven except the blasphemy against the Holy Spirit. God is clear. Speak a word against the Son of Man and you will be forgiven, but speak against the Holy Spirit and you will not be forgiven-even through eternity. (Matthew 12: 30-32)

About the Author

Larry Bailey is a freelance feature writer for various news media outlets across the country. Over the years he has taught college, served in the federal government, and worked as a broadcast news reporter. He has a BA degree in political science and a MA degree in political science from the University of Massachusetts and Temple University.

For orders contact the author at 305-283-5836
or via email at baileylb@bellsouth.net.

Made in the USA
Middletown, DE
04 November 2026

36546294R10040